15015

15015

YOUNG PEOPLE'S STORY OF
OUR HERITAGE

YOUNG PEOPLE'S STORY OF OUR HERITAGE

FINE ART

by

V. M. HILLYER and E. G. HUEY

New Edition Designed and Revised by Childrens Press, Chicago

Consultants

Ruth Esserman, Chairman, Art Department
Highland Park High School, Highland Park, Illinois

Everett Saunders, Art Lecturer, Northwestern University
Art Consultant, Wilmette School System, Wilmette, Illinois

Meredith Press, New York

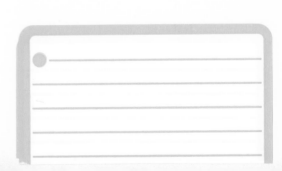

Illustrations in the order in which they appear

Library of Congress Catalog Card Number: 66-11323

Copyright © 1966 by Meredith Publishing Company. Originally published under the title of *A Child's History of Art* by V. M. Hillyer and Edward G. Huey. Copyright, 1933, by D. Appleton-Century Company, Inc. Copyright, 1951 by Appleton-Century-Crofts, Inc. Copyright, 1961 by Mercantile Safe Deposit and Trust Co. All rights reserved. Printed in the U.S.A. Published simultaneously in Canada.

Contents

Acknowledgments

Cover: **Leaping Bison,** Painting in the cave at Altamira, Spain. Rendering by John Hollis (taken from a tracing by the Abbé Henri Breuil)

Rembrandt van Rijn, **Self-Portrait,** detail
National Gallery of Art, Washington, D.C., Andrew Mellon Collection

Page 2: Murillo, **St. Joseph and the Infant Jesus,** Louvre, Paris
Alinari—Art Reference Bureau

Frontis: Hans Holbein the Younger, **Erasmus,** Louvre, Paris
Art Reference Bureau

Page 11: Painting by Bob Brunton

Opposite: Fra Filippo Lippi, **Head of the Virgin for the Painting by Badia,** Uffizi, Florence
Alinari—Art Reference Bureau

_____

Designed by John Hollis

Edited by Joan Downing Soltz

FINE ART

15,000 B.C.-1800 A.D.

The Oldest Pictures in the World

Nearly every boy and girl who has ever lived has drawn something at some time. Haven't you? You have drawn, perhaps, a horse or a house, a ship or an automobile, a dog or a cat. The dog may have looked just like a cat or a caterpillar, but even this is more than an animal can do.

Even men who lived so long ago that there were no houses, but only caves to live in, could draw. There were no paper or pencils then. Men drew pictures on the walls of their caves.

Sometimes the pictures were just scratched or cut into the wall and sometimes they were painted in afterward. The paints those men used were made of a colored clay mixed with grease, usually red or yellow. Or perhaps the paint was just blood, which was red at first and then turned almost black. Some of the pictures look as if they had been made with the end of a burned stick, as you might make a black mark with the end of a burned match. Other pictures were cut into bone—on the horns of deer or on ivory tusks.

The cave men drew pictures of only one kind of thing. Not men or women or trees or flowers or scenery. They drew chiefly pictures of animals. They were usually big animals and strange-looking to us. But they were pretty well drawn, so that we know what the animals looked like. Here is a picture like one drawn by a cave man thousands of years ago.

opposite: Wooly Mammoth. Artist's rendering after an engraving in the Les Combarelles Cave in France

It looks like an elephant and it *was* a kind of elephant—a huge elephant. But its ears were not big like our elephants' ears and it had long hair. Elephants now have skin or hide, but hardly any hair. This other animal we call a mammoth. It had long hair because the country was cold in those days and the hair kept the animal warm. And it was much, *much* bigger than the elephants we know.

There are no mammoths alive now, but men have found their bones and they have put these bones together to form huge skeletons. We still call any very big thing "mammoth." You've probably heard of Mammoth Cave in Kentucky. It was called Mammoth, not because mammoths lived in it, because they didn't, but just because it is such a huge cave.

The cave men drew other animals besides the mammoth. One was the bison, a kind of buffalo. It looks something like a bull.

Other animals they drew were like those we have now—reindeer, bears, and wolves.

Painting of a Bison, Altamira Cave, Santander

It was quite dark in the caves where the cave men drew these pictures, for of course there were no windows, and the only light was a smoky flame from a kind of lamp. Why, then, did they make pictures at all? Such pictures couldn't have been just for wall decorations, like those you may have on the walls of your home, because it was so dark in the cave. We think the pictures were made just for good luck, as some people put a horseshoe over the door for good luck. Or perhaps they were to tell a story or make a record of some animal the cave man had killed. But perhaps the cave man just had to draw something, as people today draw pictures on the walls of a shed or the telephone pad or just about anything that is handy.

The pictures made by these cave men are the oldest pictures in the world, and the artists who made them have been dead thousands of years. Can you think of anything you might ever make that would last as long as that?

Painting of a Deer, Altamira Cave, Santander

The Ancient Egyptians

The cave men made pictures on the walls and ceilings of their caves. The old Egyptians didn't live in caves. They lived in houses, where they didn't draw pictures on the walls or ceilings. Their houses were usually mud huts, not much better than the caves that the cave men lived in, but the Egyptians were not very much interested in the houses they lived in. They were much more interested in the houses they were dead in (tombs) or in the houses they made for their gods (temples).

Most dead people are buried in the ground nowadays, but the Egyptians thought the ground was no place for the dead. Besides, much of the ground of Egypt was under water for almost half of each year, for the Nile River flooded the country regularly every summer, and that would have been bad for graves.

The Egyptians believed their bodies would come to life again after thousands of years, so kings and other people who could afford it built tombs to be buried in. And they built them to last—never of wood, but of solid stone or brick. They wanted to put their bodies in a safe place. When they died, their bodies were preserved in a way we call embalming, so they would not decay.

These embalmed bodies were called mummies and the mummies were put in coffins that were shaped something like the bodies. On the coffins, or mummy cases, and on the plaster walls of their tombs and temples, the Egyptians drew and painted pictures—thousands of them, to cover every bit of space.

These pictures that the Egyptians made on the mummy cases and on the walls of tombs and temples were not pictures of wild animals such as the cave men made. Some were of animals, though not the kind of animals the cave men drew. Most of the pictures were of people—men and women, kings and queens, gods and goddesses.

Some Egyptian pictures seem to have something wrong with them. Can you tell what's wrong with either of the pictures on page nineteen?

It's this: the eyes have the shape an eye has when we see it from the front, but the faces are side faces or profiles. So they are front eyes in profiles.

Another peculiar thing about these pictures is that the bodies are twisted. The shoulders are full front, but the hips, legs, and feet are sideways.

In old Egyptian times all the artists drew certain things in a certain way. The artists were taught to draw that way, and they had to draw that way such things as I have mentioned—the front eye in the profile, the front shoulders with a side view of legs and feet.

We call pictures that tell a story illustrations. Egyptian pictures are chiefly illustrations. They tell a story either with or without words—a story of the life of some dead king or queen, their battles, their hunting parties, their parades. And above, below, or at the side, there are often words, in Egyptian writing, that describe the pictures. These words look very much like pictures, themselves, for the Egyptian writing is a kind of picture writing. It is called hieroglyphics.

When Egyptian artists drew a king with common people around him, they made the king very large and the other people very small. The king was made to be a giant—two or three times as large as the common people—just to show he was really a *great* man.

When the Egyptian artists drew pictures of crowds, they didn't know how to show men farther back in the picture by drawing them smaller and raising them a little bit. They made those farther back the same size as those in front, and to show that they *were* farther back they put those in the back *above* those in front

We have hundreds of colors and shades nowadays, but the Egyptians had only four bright colors—red, yellow, green, blue. Besides these they had black, white, and brown. And their colors lasted. These pictures the Egyptians made are almost as fresh and bright as when they were first done thousands of years ago. That's partly because the pictures were hidden away in the dark where the sun could not fade them. They were drawn and painted on the plaster walls and the colors were very bright—not like nature. It didn't matter whether something really had any color, or what the particular color should be. They painted it the way they thought looked well.

When you think of all these old pictures that were not meant to be seen by the eye of any man, you may wonder why the Egyptians made them. What was the idea? And yet today when we build a great building we put into a hollow stone in the foundation—a cornerstone—the daily paper, photographs of people alive at the time, and so on. Why? The building is expected to last for ages and the cornerstone will never be opened until the building comes down. Our idea may be something like the old Egyptians' idea, after all!

upper right: Egyptian Wall Painting, **Fowling in the Marshes,** from the Tomb of Nebaum, Thebes, about 1400 B.C., British Museum, London

lower right: Egyptian Wall Painting, **Festival of Sekhtet,** from the Tomb of Nakht, Thebes, about 1410 B.C., British Museum, London

Artists of the
Two River Country

An inch away from Egypt on my map, but a thousand miles away on the ground, was another old country called—well, there were several countries there. Egypt was a country with one river. These other countries, a thousand miles off to the east, had two rivers, so let's bunch them together and call them, for short, the Two River Country. The real names of these countries were Mesopotamia, Chaldea, Babylonia, and Assyria. Egypt and the Two River Country are among the oldest civilizations in the world.

Here in this Two River Country once were the largest and most important cities of the ancient world—cities bigger, perhaps, than New York or London—and here ruled mighty kings. Yet there isn't a building of these old cities left. The reason for this is that the buildings weren't built of stone as the buildings of Egypt were, for there was very little stone in the Two River Country. They were built of bricks made of mud, of which there was plenty, but the bricks were only dried in the sun, not baked by fire as the Egyptian bricks were. These buildings made of sun-dried bricks have all crumbled away, and where once were magnificent cities there are now only mounds of brick dust that look like natural hills.

You may wonder why the people of these countries didn't bake their bricks in fire, for fire-baked bricks last longer than almost anything else. The reason is that they didn't have much wood or much other fuel to make fire with. On some bricks, however, they painted pictures and decorations and these they covered with a glass-like substance (glaze), then baked them in the fire so that they became colored tiles. These tiles have lasted and have been found by men digging down in the mounds that once were cities of brick buildings.

In Egypt, as I told you, the artists painted pictures chiefly for the dead to see. In the Two River Country artists didn't care about the dead people. They painted pictures for live people to see.

The kings didn't build tombs. They weren't interested in what was to become of them after they were dead. Instead, they built great palaces for themselves and great temples for their gods. These palaces and temples were built of brick, but a mud palace or temple was not very beautiful, so the artists covered the walls with pictures made on slabs of alabaster and with tiles.

Alabaster is a stone, usually white, so soft that it can be cut easily. So the artists cut pictures on slabs of alabaster and painted them in much the same way that the Egyptians painted their pictures.

Each tile had on it a different part of a picture, and then a great many tiles were put together to form a large picture, as picture puzzles are put together from separate pieces. There is a kind of picture, which you may have seen, that is made of many tiny pieces of different colored stones or tiles. A picture made this way is called a mosaic, and the people who lived in the Two River Country were the first to use a kind of mosaic work.

The Egyptian pictures on the inside walls of the tombs or temples are still there, but those on the mummy cases have been put in museums. The alabaster and tile pictures of the Two River people were dug up from under the mounds that once were buildings and they too have been put in museums.

These alabaster and tile pictures made in the Two River Country told stories about the king and his courtiers. The two chief things the king and his courtiers did were to hunt wild animals and to fight battles, so there were many pictures of battles and hunting parties.

The pictures found in the Two River Country are like the Egyptian pictures in some ways. As in Egypt, the eye is a front eye in a profile, but the shoulders are drawn side view. When an artist wished to show men behind those in front, he drew the figures *above* those in front as the Egyptian artists did. But in some of their pictures the Two River artists did try to show the men behind by raising them only a little in the picture and making them smaller, and by partly covering those behind with those in front. This effect, showing distance in a picture, is called perspective.

Assyrian Rosettes

Assyrian Tree of Life

Tree of Life from
relief column of topes,
Sanchi, State of Bhophal, India

But the kind of men the Two River artists drew were different from those the Egyptians drew. The Two River artists admired strength and strong men, and they thought all strong men had long hair and beards. So they made the pictures of kings very muscular, with bulging muscles in their arms and legs, and with long hair and long beards which were carefully curled into corkscrew curls.

The pictures of animals these people made are much more natural than those the Egyptians drew. The ones they liked best to paint were the lion and the bull, because these animals are so strong.

The Two River people were especially good at making designs and decorations for borders. One was called the rosette. It is a dot with a little wheel-like arrangement around it; we are still using this design. Another design they made was called the guilloche, which we pronounce gee-lōsh'. We use some of the same designs today in tiles for bathroom floors and for the halls of public buildings.

One picture the Two River people made has been copied by the artists of many other countries. This was an ornamental design called the Tree of Life. It is a tree like no tree that grows. It has many different kinds of leaves and flowers and fruits all on the same tree at the same time. It is often used in designs on rugs and in embroidery.

The Lost Paintings
of Greece

_____

When I was a boy, there used to be a candy shop on the corner. On the counter was painted a silver dollar. It was painted so naturally that every one tried to pick it up. I thought it wonderful and that the artist who had done it must be a wonderful artist, too.

I remember also being taken to an art gallery where there was one picture that I liked best. To me it was a marvel. It was the picture of a door half open, with a lady peeking out from behind it. When you first looked at it, you were startled. The picture was so lifelike you could hardly believe it was not a real person looking out from behind a real door. I thought that must be the greatest kind of art—to paint something so natural and lifelike that a person would be fooled into thinking it real.

The old Greek painters seemed to feel the same way about pictures. Greece is across the Mediterranean Sea from Egypt. The Greeks were among the greatest sculptors who have ever lived and were also great architects. But their pictures were not so great, for many of them were of this kind of "April Fool" painting that I've described. They tried to paint pictures that would fool people into believing they were real.

In Egypt and Assyria we know the paintings but not the names of the painters who did them. In Greece we know the names of the painters but not the paintings they did. The first Greek painter whose name we do know was Polygnotus. He is called the father of Greek painting. The writers of the time of Polygnotus tell us that he was a wonderful painter, but not one of his pictures is in existence, so we have to take their word for it.

As a matter of fact, we have very few Greek paintings, and one reason that we have so few is that most of the pictures were painted on something that could be moved from place to place, like the pictures we hang on our own walls, and these movable pictures have all been lost or destroyed.

One of the most famous Greek painters was an artist named Zeuxis, who lived four hundred years before Christ was born. It is said that he painted a boy carrying a bunch of grapes and the grapes looked so real that the birds came and pecked at them, trying to eat them. He entered his picture in a contest, or match, with a rival painter named Parrhasius. It was to be decided which was the better artist. Everyone was sure that Zeuxis must get the prize because the birds were fooled into thinking the grapes he had painted were real. Parrhasius's picture had a curtain drawn across the front of it.

"Now," said Zeuxis to Parrhasius, "draw back the curtain and show us your picture."

To which Parrhasius replied: "The curtain *is* my picture. Even you, a human being, were fooled into thinking it was real. So I win. You fooled the birds, but I fooled you. And besides, the boy you painted holding the grapes wasn't so lifelike or he would have scared the birds away."

The greatest of all the Greek painters was named Apelles. He was a great friend of the young ruler and general, Alexander the Great, and painted Alexander's portrait. And yet we know this artist better for two of his sayings that have become famous than for his pictures.

A shoemaker once criticized the way Apelles had painted a sandal in one of his pictures. Apelles was glad to have expert advice from one who knew sandals and he made the correction. The next day the shoemaker criticized another part of the same picture. But this time Apelles did not like the criticism, for he felt the shoemaker didn't know what he was talking about, so he exclaimed, "Let the shoemaker stick to his last," which meant, let him stick to his own business, to things he knows about.

Apelles was a very hard worker and made it a rule never to let a day go by without doing some worth-while work. So he used to say, "No day without a line." Though it is more than two thousand years since he lived, we still quote these sayings. They have become proverbs. They have lasted, but none of his paintings have, though everyone who lived at his time honored him and called him the greatest painter of Greece.

Greek Painting on Jars, Jugs, and Vases

One kind of Greek painting has lasted, examples of which are in many museums. These are the paintings that were made on vases.

Greek vases were all made out of clay and they were not used for flowers as our vases usually are. They were used to hold anything liquid—water, wine, oil, ointments, perfumes—as we would use jars and jugs, bottles and bowls, cups and kettles, pitchers or tin cans. They were made in many beautiful shapes. Some were tall and thin, some were short and fat. Some had one handle like a cup, some had two handles. Our pitchers and kettles and bowls today, whether they are made of glass or silver or china, are copies of many of the Greek vase forms. The Greeks had names for most of the shapes, and though the names are hard, you might like to learn some of them.

The *kylix* was a flat vase, shaped something like a fruit dish.

The *askos* was a low vase with a spout and a handle across the top. It was used for oil with which to fill lamps. It was, in other words, an oil can—only it was not made of tin.

The *amphora* was a rather fat vase with two handles.

The *oinochoe* was a pitcher-shaped vase.

The *lekythos* was a tall, thin, bottle-shaped vase with one handle.

All the better vases were painted on the outside, with pictures. The pictures were not of kings and queens. In Egypt, the kings and queens would have been pictured. In Assyria, there would have been pictures of kings. But at that time the Greeks had no royalty, and no use for kings and queens. So they painted Greek gods and Greek heroes and scenes from their fairy tales or mythology. Many of these pictures on the vases are like illustrations in a book and are very graceful.

The pictures were usually in two styles. In the first style, they were painted black or dark on a reddish flower-pot or clay-color background. In the second style, the background was black and the pictures were reddish or clay color as if the whole vase had been painted black, then the picture scraped out so the clay color was left to form the picture.

above: Greek Vase
Oinochoe from Aegina
British Museum, London

───────────

upper left: Greek Vases,
Kylix and Askos,
British Museum, London

───────────

lower left: Greek Vases
Amphora and Lekythos
British Museum, London

Twelfth-Century Mosaic. **Christ Pantocrator,** detail, Cathedral, Cefalù

Early Christian Art

One of the names we know best, in all history, is that of Christ, and yet no one knows what he looked like. More paintings have been made of him than of any man who has ever lived, but they are all imaginary, for the earliest picture of him was made long after the time when he lived. It was painted by artists who never saw him, so they had to guess how he looked.

The greatest city in the world at the time of Christ was Rome, Italy, and soon there were more Christians in Rome than in the country where Christ was born and lived. The early Christians were a secret society. Their society had to be secret, because the rulers of the people thought them dangerous and tortured them and even put them to death.

So the Christian society in Rome cut tunnels and cellar-like rooms—thousands of them—underneath the ground and there they held meetings. They were buried there, too, in places cut into the walls. These dark, damp caves, lighted only with small, dim lamps, were called catacombs. On the ceilings and sides of the catacombs the Christians painted pictures. One was a picture of Christ as the good shepherd, carrying a sheep across his shoulders. And where do you suppose they got the face they used for Christ? It was the picture of a Greek god!

Other pictures those early Christians painted were of Daniel in the lion's den, Jonah and the whale, and the Greek god Orpheus charming the wild animals with his magic music.

But most of the paintings in the catacombs were not what you would call real pictures. They were decorations, but decorations that had some meaning to Christians. They made pictures of a dove because that represented the Holy Ghost, which they believed came down from heaven in the form of a dove. They painted the cock that was supposed to have crowed when Peter denied that he knew Christ. They painted an anchor which meant that their religion was like any other that kept a boat in a storm from being dashed on the rocks. The anchor was their safeguard.

About three hundred years after Christ died, a Roman emperor named Constantine became a Christian himself. Then, for the first time, the Christian society no longer needed to be secret. The Christians had no further fear of harm, so they came out of the catacombs to do their worshiping openly and built churches aboveground and covered the walls with pictures and mosaics. Then for over a thousand years they painted pictures of people and scenes from the Bible.

The Greeks painted pictures chiefly of people without any clothes on, because they thought the human figure the most beautiful thing in the world and they did not want to cover it up. The Christian painters thought such figures immodest, and in the pictures they made they covered up the entire body with clothing, so that only the face, hands, and feet showed. They spent all their efforts in trying to make the face soulful and holy—not just beautiful. Often the background was painted in gold. Sometimes the pictures, instead of being painted, were made of mosaic. Paintings on plaster walls would peel and crumble and rub off, but mosaic would last. Mosaic pictures were often made on the floors of churches because such a picture made of stones was the only kind that would stand the tread of countless feet.

Some of the best paintings the Christian artists made were tiny illustrations or decorations for their Bibles and holy books. Some of these pictures were no larger than a postage stamp. Most of them were made by the monks, pious men who gave their lives to the service of the Church. All books were written by hand (we call them manuscripts), for printing had not been invented. These pictures for books were called illuminations and were made in gold and bright colors.

First page of the Gospel of Luke from a twelfth-century Armenian illuminated manuscript containing the four gospels.

Cimabue and Giotto

The father of Greek painting, you may remember, was a man named Polygnotus. About two thousand years later, there lived a man who is called the father of Italian painting. His name is Cimabue—pronounced Chee-ma-boo'ay. Cimabue lived in Florence, which means the City of Flowers. It is in the central part of Italy. There are very few of his paintings in existence, and we are not sure that certain pictures are really his. And you may not see from the paintings we have why he was supposed to be such a great painter.

If Cimabue were painting now, probably he would not be considered great, but in his time he was thought very great, because he was so much better than any other painter had been for a thousand years before him. When he had finished painting a large picture of the Virgin Mary, it is said the people of Florence thought it so beautiful they formed a procession and, with trumpets sounding and banners flying carried the picture through the streets from his house to the church where it was placed.

Another picture that Cimabue painted is of a monk, Saint Francis. Monks were holy men who spent their whole time in trying to be good and in doing good. Saint Francis started a society of monks called after him, Franciscans. Those who joined the society promised to try to live as Christ had lived. They could own nothing, they could have no money. They could not marry. They spent all their time doing good. They worked to earn their daily bread and lodging. They shaved the top of their heads, leaving a circular place bare like a bald spot, and kept it shaved so that every one would know they were monks. This shaved circle was called a tonsure. They wore a rough brown robe with a hood, and they held the robe together with a coarse rope tied around the waist.

The circle Cimabue painted around Saint Francis's head is called a halo. A halo was painted around the heads of saints to show that they were holy persons. The spots on this saint's hands are not an accident. It is said Saint Francis wanted so to be like Christ that an angel came to him and made on his hands and feet nail holes like those that Christ had received on the cross. Those nail marks are called stigmata.

But it is not for what he did himself that Cimabue is famous. He is known chiefly as the teacher of someone who became a much greater artist. Cimabue was walking one day in the country, not far from Florence, when he came upon a shepherd boy tending his flocks. The boy, while watching his sheep, was drawing pictures of them on a piece of slate with a sharp stone. Cimabue, looking over the boy's shoulder, was amazed at the picture he saw and he asked the boy his name. "Giotto," the boy replied, which was the short pet name for Ambro*giotto*.

Cimabue asked Giotto if he wouldn't like to go to Florence and study drawing and painting. The boy was delighted to have such a chance. So, getting permission from his father, he went to live and study with Cimabue. When Giotto grew up, he painted many famous pictures of Christ, the Virgin Mary, and especially of Saint Francis.

Saint Francis lived in a town near Florence called Assisi. In Assisi there is a church built in his honor. In fact, there are two churches, one on top of the other. In the upper church, Giotto painted along the walls a series of pictures that told stories from the life of Saint Francis. One of the many wonderful things Saint Francis did was preach sermons to the birds that gathered round him to listen. One of Giotto's paintings shows him doing this.

In those days, the paint used was not like that we have now. The paint we use is usually made by mixing colored powder with oil (we call it oil paint), and artists paint pictures on canvas. But in those days, oil was not used in making paint, and the painting was not done on canvas. Artists mixed their powdered colors with water and painted on fresh plastered walls. This kind of painting, on fresh plaster, was called fresco, which means fresh. Or they mixed their colors with something sticky, like egg or glue, and painted on dry plaster, wood, or copper. This kind of painting was called tempera, which means mixed.

The story is told that the pope wished to have a picture painted and sent a messenger to Giotto to ask for a sample of the artist's work. Giotto dipped his brush in some paint and, with a single swinging stroke, painted a perfect circle on a piece of wood and sent this to the pope to show how skilled he was. Do you think you could draw a perfect circle without a compass with one stroke of a pencil? Try it. Then try doing it with a brush.

But even if you can do this, it does not mean you are a great artist. It is easy to trace a drawing. It is not much harder to copy a drawing without tracing. Thousands of people can paint a basket of fruit, a vase of flowers, a view of the sea or the land. That is just a copy. Thousands can copy the painting of a great artist so well that you can hardly tell the copy from the original. But very few people are able to *invent* a picture out of their own heads and put the parts together to make a beautiful painting. That is what takes genius!

opposite left: Giotto, **St. Francis Preaching to the Birds,**
Upper Church of S. Francesco, Assisi

---

opposite right: Cimabue, **St. Francis**, detail,
Lower Church of S. Francesco, Assisi

35

Fra Angelico,
The Angel-Like Brother

The buildings in which monks live together are called monasteries. The monks are known as "brothers" because they are supposed to treat one another and every one else like brothers.

In Florence, the City of Flowers, was a monastery called St. Mark's, for the apostle who wrote the second book of the New Testament. In this monastery of St. Mark's lived a monk who, because he was so very good and holy, was called the Angel-like Brother. In his language, which was Italian, Brother Angel-like was Fra Angelico. It may seem strange that a monk should become a great artist, but Fra Angelico had a talent for drawing and painting and he painted Bible pictures on the walls of the rooms in his monastery.

above left: Fra Angelico, **Annunciation**
Museo San Marco, Florence

---

below left: Fra Angelico, **St. Peter Martyr**
Museo San Marco, Florence

The rooms where the monks slept were called cells because they were so plain and bare that they were almost like cells in a prison. There were forty of these cells and Fra Angelico spent most of his life painting them so that the monks would have scenes from the Bible to look at and think about. These pictures were painted in fresco. Besides these, Fra Angelico painted movable pictures on wooden panels in tempera, which, as I have told you, was color mixed with something sticky, like egg or glue.

Fra Angelico lived about a hundred years later than Giotto, but his style was very much like Giotto's style. It is said that always before starting to paint a picture, he prayed long and earnestly. Then when he did set to work on a painting, he never changed a brush stroke, but left everything he did just as he first put it down. For he believed that the Lord had guided his hand, and that therefore no correction should be made.

There was one religious subject that painters of that time loved to paint. It is called the annunciation. The Bible says that an angel came to Mary and told her that she was to have a son who was to be Christ the Lord. This is called the annunciation—that is, the *announcement* to Mary that she was to be the mother of the Lord. Fra Angelico painted an annunciation which I think you'll agree is very beautiful. In this picture, Mary is seated on a stool on the porch of her home, with her arms folded across her breast. An angel messenger who has just descended from heaven, half kneels to tell Mary that she is to have a divine son.

The monks of St. Mark's were not allowed to talk to one another except at certain times, as a special treat. They had to keep silent most of the time. Think of keeping silent, for one single day, or even for one hour, if there were anyone around to talk to! That rule was made so that the monks might keep their thoughts always on God and religion and not waste their time in gossip or other worthless talk. Over a doorway in St. Mark's monastery, Fra Angelico painted a picture of Saint Peter with his finger on his lips, to remind the monks that they must be silent.

The monastery of St. Mark's has been made a museum for the paintings of Fra Angelico. It now contains most of his movable paintings as well as the fresco paintings on the cell walls. One of these movable paintings now in the St. Mark's monastery is a picture of Mary with the Christ Child. Mary is called "My Lady," and this, in Italian, is Madonna. So such a picture is called a Madonna.

For hundreds of years, thousands of pictures of the Madonna were painted. In fact, nearly every artist painted at least one Madonna and often many Madonnas. Each church had to have one or more Madonnas. And every family that could afford to have any painting at all had a Madonna hanging on the walls.

The Madonna that Fra Angelico painted is in a broad gold frame. Often the frame of a picture is just a frame—a fence to separate it from the wall and other things on the wall—and has no beauty in itself. But on this particular frame, Fra Angelico painted twelve angels playing musical instruments.

The old Egyptians believed they would come to life again in a thousand years perhaps, after they had died. The old Greeks didn't think much about coming to life again, but about two thousand years after the old Greek artists had died, people were born in Italy who in many ways were like those old Greeks. Indeed, these Italians were so like the old Greeks that it seemed almost as if the old Greeks had been born again, and were living once more—not in Greece, but in Italy. So we call this time the Renaissance (Ren'uh-sahns), which means "born again."

One of the first artists of the Renaissance was a boy who had a very insulting nickname. Now, nicknames stick to some people when they grow up. But it seems strange that this boy, who became a great painter, was always called by his insulting nickname. To this very day we know him by the name Masaccio (Ma-zat'cho). In Italian it means "Dirty Tom."

Early Italian Renaissance Painters

Masaccio was a very poor boy and he died young. When he died he was still very poor and still very dirty. No one seemed to like him or his painting while he lived and some people even say he was poisoned by his enemies. But after he died, people thought differently about him. Great artists thought his paintings so good that they went to the place where they could be seen, to study and copy them.

The reason other artists studied and copied his pictures is that Masaccio had found out how to do something that no artist before him had been able to do. Masaccio's pictures did not look flat. He painted pictures so that you could see back *into* them. Perspective, you remember, we call it.

For thousands of years artists had tried to get perspective, but they had not succeeded very well. One of Masaccio's famous frescoes was *The Tribute Money.*

Fra Filippo Lippi, **Madonna and Child with St. John,**
Uffizi, Florence

41

One of the painters who studied Masaccio's frescoes was a monk named Fra Filippo Lippi—that is, Brother Filippo, which means Philip, though it is spelled with an *F* instead of *Ph*. Brother Filippo was, however, not a good and holy monk like that religious painter, Brother Angelico. Brother Filippo was a good painter, but a bad brother. It is said that he was bored with being good and with being a monk, so he ran away from his monastery. After many wild adventures, he was captured by pirates and made a slave. One day he drew with a piece of charcoal a picture of his master. The likeness was so good that his master set him free.

Brother Filippo made his way back to Italy and was hired to paint a picture of the Madonna for a convent. A convent is a building where nuns live. Nuns have given up their lives to religion; they live together as monks do in a monastery.

One of the nuns in this convent, a beautiful young girl, posed as the model for Filippo's painting of the Virgin. Now, neither a monk nor a nun is supposed to fall in love with any one, but, in spite of what he was supposed *not* to do, Filippo fell in love with the nun and, in spite of everything, they ran away together. They had a son whom they named Filippino, which means "Little Filippo." Filippino became a great painter, too—even greater than his father.

Another artist of this time has a name—or rather two names—I like to say because each name has "ozzo" in it, a kind of rhyme. It is Benozzo Gozzoli (Ben-ot′zo Gotz′o-lē).

In the city of Pisa is a peculiar tower that does not stand straight, but leans to one side. In the same city is another peculiar thing. It is a cemetery. The peculiar thing about this cemetery is that the ground for it was brought all the way from Jerusalem so that the earth in which people were buried would be especially holy—the same ground that Christ had trod. It took fifty-three shiploads of this holy earth to make the cemetery. It is called the Campo Santo, which means Holy Field.

Around the Campo Santo is a wall and on the inside of this wall Benozzo Gozzoli painted scenes from the Old Testament —the story of Noah, the Tower of Babel, David, Solomon,

Masaccio, **The Tribute Money,** detail,
Santa Maria del Carmine, Florence

———

and so on—twenty-two of them. There were crowds of people in each picture and often buildings in the back of the picture.

In most of the pictures that Benozzo Gozzoli painted, as well as in those of other painters of this time, the clothing of the people was not the kind of clothing the people of Bible times wore. And the buildings in the background were not those of Bible times or places at all. The artists had not visited Bible lands and didn't know what kind of clothes the people wore or what kind of buildings they built, so they made the clothes and buildings like the Italian clothes and buildings of their own time.

So here are three painters to begin the early Renaissance, the hundred years from 1400 to 1500. These three painters may not seem to you much like old Greeks born again, but be sure to remember them—Masaccio, Fra Filippo Lippi, and Benozzo Gozzoli, who lived and worked just before Columbus discovered America.

43

Alessandro Botticelli, **Primavera (The Allegory of Spring),** Uffizi, Florence

The Beginning of the High Renaissance

One of the first dates that every American boy and girl learns is 1492, the year that Columbus discovered America. Columbus was an Italian, but most of the people in Italy at that time

Alessandro Botticelli,
**Madonna of the Magnificat
(Madonna of the Coronation),**
Uffizi, Florence

were not interested in Columbus or what he was doing. They were interested in just two things. First they were interested in having a good time. The second thing they were interested in was art. They were interested in Greece and its art and learning—not in discovering new countries. This time was known as the beginning of the High Renaissance and began just about 1492.

When you look at a globe of the world, it is hard to find Italy, no larger than your little finger, jutting down into the Mediterranean Sea. And yet in this little finger of land lived, at the time we are talking about, the greatest artists there have ever been. We call these artists the old masters. It may seem strange that just there in Italy the greatest artists should have been born and lived, all within a few miles of one another. One explanation is that Italy was the center of the Christian religion, and up to this time Italian artists painted no pictures but religious ones.

Fra Bartolommeo, **Savonarola,** Museo San Marco, Florence

An artist named Botticelli (Bot-tee-chel′lee), was one of the first Italian artists to paint pictures of things that were not told about in the Bible. Botticelli painted religious pictures too, but he liked especially to paint pictures of Greek gods and goddesses. Botticelli had a peculiar style of painting. His women usually had long legs and seemed to be dancing or floating along the ground instead of standing or walking. They were clad in very filmy, gauzy gowns. One of his pictures is called *The Allegory of Spring.*

46

Now, at the time of Columbus, there was living and preaching in Florence a monk named Savonarola, who some people think was mad. At any rate, he was such a powerful preacher that those who heard his sermons would do almost anything he told them to. He seemed to hypnotize them. Many of the people in Florence were very wicked. They thought of nothing but pleasure and having a good time, no matter how bad they were when they had a good time. Savonarola preached against the sins of this world, and prophesied death for those who did not repent and mend their ways. He preached against people who played games of cards or dice, who used rouge on their faces, who wore ornaments, who danced, who sang songs that were not hymns, or wrote books or painted pictures that were not religious. The people of Florence began to repent and one day they brought all their ornaments and finery and fancy clothes and bad books to the public square and made a huge bonfire of them. It was much higher than a house. Many ugly things were burned up—probably most of them ought to have been burned. But many very good books and works of art were burned, too.

Botticelli had heard Savonarola preach, and he felt that he had committed a sin in painting pictures of gods and goddesses and other subjects that were not religious. So he brought his paintings that were not religious and threw them on the bonfire. Fortunately for us, only a few of Botticelli's pictures were burned and his best ones are still preserved in art galleries.

One of his religious pictures is a Madonna that is circular in shape, not square-cornered as most pictures are. Circular pictures are called *tondos*, which means round.

This one is called *The Madonna of the Coronation* (the crowning), because two angels are putting a crown on Mary to show that she is the queen of heaven. She is writing a song in a book while the infant Jesus seems to be guiding her hand. The song sung in church today is called the Magnificat because that is the Latin name, and so the picture too is often called *The Magnificat*. The song is a thanksgiving to God that he has chosen Mary from among all the women in the world to be the mother of Jesus.

The boy holding the inkwell and the one holding the book were real boys. They did not live in the time of Christ, but in the time of Botticelli, so it may seem strange that they should have been put in the picture. But the old masters often did that sort of thing. When these two boys grew up both of them became popes.

Eventually, the people Savonarola said were so wicked could stand him no longer, and even some of his own followers turned against him. Finally they hanged him on a cross placed in the public square. Then, not satisfied with that, they burned his body at the stake. And not satisfied with that, they threw his ashes into the river.

There was a young painter in Florence who, as Botticelli had done, had burned all of his pictures that were not religious. He was so shocked by the way in which Savonarola had been treated that he gave up painting and became a monk himself. He took the name Fra Bartolommeo and went to live in the monastery where Savonarola had lived and where Fra Angelico before him had lived—the monastery of St. Mark's. For six years he never painted a stroke or touched a brush. He did nothing but pray. Then he was persuaded to start painting once more, and after that he made many beautiful pictures—all of them, of course, religious. One picture he painted was of a saint named Sebastian. Saint Sebastian was shot to death with arrows, because he was a Christian. The picture which Fra Bartolommeo painted for his monastery showed Saint Sebastian without clothes and with arrows sticking in his body. The monks thought this so immodest that at last the picture was removed from the monastery.

Fra Bartolommeo painted a picture of his hero Savonarola. Savonarola was not handsome at all. In fact, he had a very big nose, and was really ugly, so ugly that his enemies used to joke about it. But the painting of him that Fra Bartolommeo made shows that a picture can be great without being pretty. Fra Bartolommeo didn't change Savonarola's features at all. He painted the man just as he was, but the picture is beautiful because it shows someone who bore the most terrible suffering and agony for what he believed was right.

Most artists, when they draw or paint pictures of people, have real men or women to pose for them. Models, we call them. Instead of live models, Fra Bartolommeo used a wooden jointed doll which he dressed and arranged in the position he wanted the figure to be. Such a wooden doll is called a lay-figure or one to draw from.

Fra Bartolommeo was the first painter to put baby angels at the foot of his pictures of the Madonna, and other painters copied this idea.

Fra Bartolommeo, **Head of a Baby**

Historical Pictures Service, Chicago

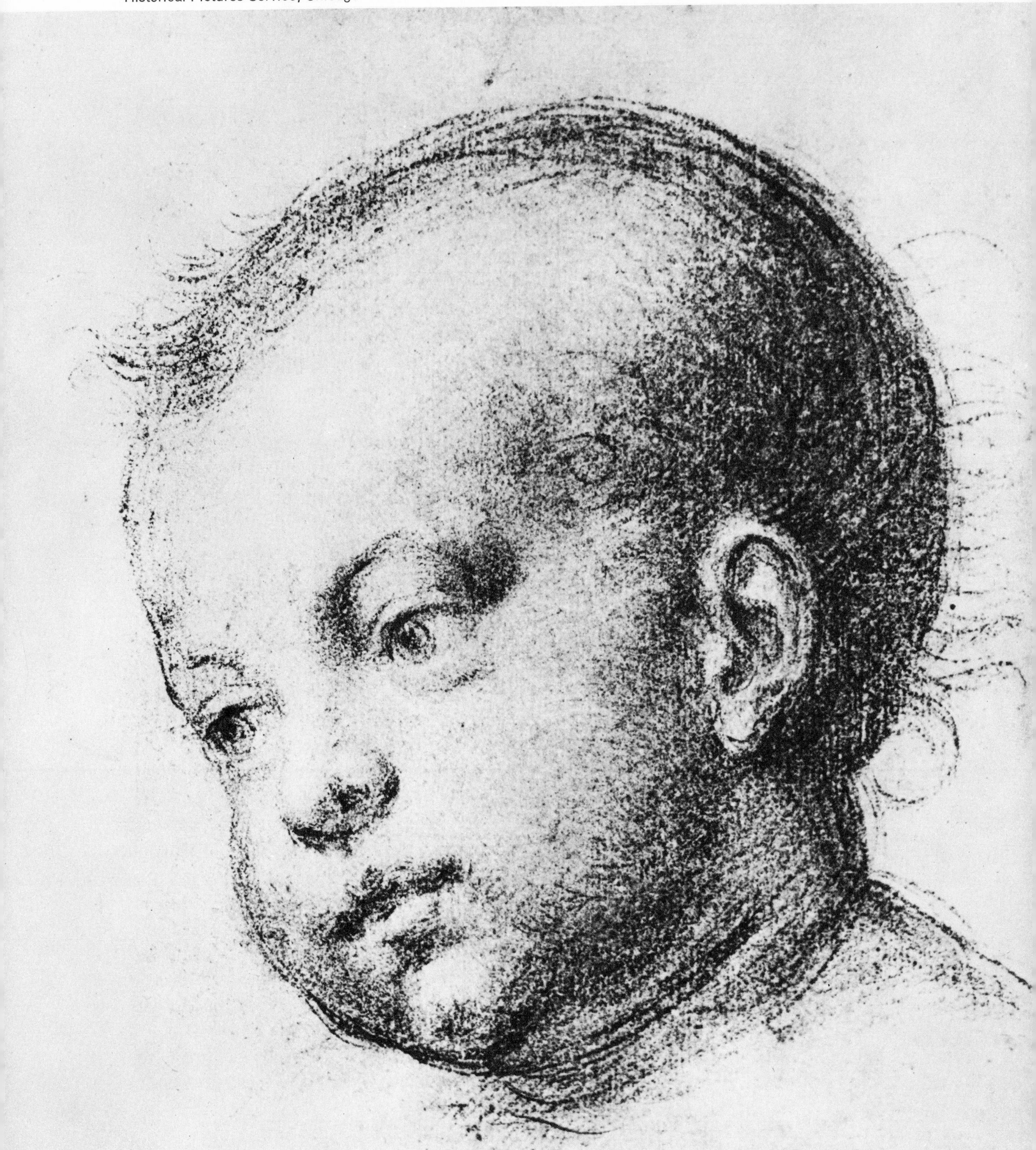

More Renaissance Painters

Many towns are named for persons. It is not so often that persons are named for towns, but here is a painter who was named for one. The town was Perugia, in Italy, and the man was called Perugino (Pay-roo-jee'no). He wasn't christened Perugino, but most people have forgotten what his real name was. Perugino wasn't even born in Perugia, but he went to live in that town and started a school for painters there.

You can tell whom some letters are from before you open them, just by the handwriting on the envelope. In the same way you can tell a picture that Perugino has painted even if it hasn't his name on it. He painted Madonnas and saints and after you have seen several of them, you can recognize others he did, even though you may not be able to tell just how or why. Usually they have their heads bent to one side, a very sweet expression, and usually the figure has one knee bent.

Perugino painted many beautiful pictures, but he is chiefly famous because of one of his pupils. This pupil was a boy many people feel became the greatest painter of all time. His name is Raphael. Raphael studied with Perugino for three years. By the time he was nineteen years old he had learned everything that his master could teach him, so he started out for himself. He died when he was thirty-seven years old, but he was such a hard worker that he had painted or drawn over a thousand pictures by that time. Indeed, we are told that he died from overwork.

Raphael must have done about one picture a week, and some of his paintings are very large and have many figures in them. The only way he could have made so many, and the way we know he did, was to have his pupils help him. He always painted the faces himself, but his pupils painted the clothes and hands and other less important parts of the pictures.

It would take several books with a picture on each page to show all of Raphael's paintings. One of the most famous is

Perugino, **S. Maria Maddalena,** Galleria Pitti, Florence

Perugino, **The Crucifixion with the Virgin, St. John, St. Jerome, and St. Mary Magdalen**

Raphael, **Madonna del Gran Duca,** Galleria Pitti, Florence

Art Reference Bureau

53

The Madonna del Gran Duca. It was called this because it was bought by a grand duke who prized it more highly than all his riches. In fact, he was not willing to have it hanging on the wall of his palace or placed in a vault for safekeeping. He wanted it with him all the time and is said to have carried it with him in his carriage wherever he went so that it would never be out of his sight. The grand duke is now dead, of course, and *The Madonna del Gran Duca* is in an art gallery. How fortunate, you may think, are the people who live near an art gallery. They may see great paintings every day without cost. Yet I know people living near great galleries who have never been inside them. Strange? That seems to be the way with people. Some people go thousands of miles and pay thousands of dollars to get to a fine gallery, while those who live almost next door don't or won't "go across the street" to see the paintings there.

Raphael painted another Madonna called *The Madonna of the Chair.* It is a tondo. Do you remember what that is? It is a round picture.

The story is that Raphael was walking one day in the country when he saw a young mother sitting in a doorway with her little baby.

"What a beautiful madonna!" Raphael said to himself. "I must paint her now, on the spot where she is, before she changes."

He looked around for something to paint on and, in a rubbish heap near by, he saw the round top of a barrel. So he sketched the young woman and her baby then and there with a pencil. And as soon as he reached his home he made the painting of them.

But the most famous picture in the world is another Madonna by Raphael called *The Sistine Madonna* or *Madonna di Sansisto* from the name of the church where it was first placed. It was later placed in a gallery in Dresden, Germany, where it

---

Raphael, **The Sistine Madonna (Madonna di Sansisto)**
Galerie, Dresden

has a room all by itself, for no other picture was thought worthy to be hung in the same room.

Many Madonnas that I have mentioned may be beautiful themselves, but the child in the pictures may not be beautiful at all. He often looks like a little old man or just a very fat baby, and not a bit what we feel he should look like. The Christ Child in Raphael's *Sistine Madonna* is very beautiful. Leaning on the edge of the frame, beneath the feet of the Madonna, are two little angels or cherubs. This idea Raphael got from Fra Bartolommeo, who was a great friend of his. The two other people in the picture who are worshiping the Madonna are Pope Sixtus and Saint Barbara. They, of course, did not live at the time of Christ. They were put in this picture just as Botticelli put two living boys into his picture of the Coronation.

Michelangelo, the Sculptor who Painted Pictures

At the time of the Renaissance, young girls used to wear golden garlands or wreaths around their hair, as girls today wear bracelets round their wrists or rings on their fingers. One goldsmith was so famous for the garlands he made that he was called Ghirlandajo (Gear-lan-dah'yo), which means a maker of garlands. Ghirlandajo gave up making garlands and began to paint pictures instead. He made many very fine pictures, but the chief thing he did was teach an artist, Michelangelo (Mike-el-an'je-lo). Michelangelo studied with Ghirlandajo for three years, and the teacher paid the pupil, instead of charging for his teaching!

above: Michelangelo, **The Holy Family (The Doni Madonna),** Uffizi, Florence

Left: Michelangelo, **A Philosopher,** pen and ink, British Museum, London

overleaf: Michelangelo, **Creation of Man,** Sistine Chapel, Vatican, Rome

Ghirlandajo was probably a good teacher of painting, but young Michelangelo liked making statues better than painting pictures. So he left Ghirlandajo's workshop and began to study sculpture.

Michelangelo soon became famous as a sculptor—a man who makes statues or sculpture. He moved from the city of Florence to Rome, and there he worked for the pope, who liked Michelangelo's work so much that he didn't want him to make statues for anyone else.

This pope wanted to have pictures painted on the ceiling of the Sistine Chapel in Rome. The Sistine is a chapel in the Vatican, the palace of the popes. It has a very high curved ceiling. The pope asked Michelangelo to paint the pictures on the ceiling, but the artist said that he was a sculptor and didn't at all want to paint. Then some enemies of his spread around the story that he didn't want to do it because he wasn't good enough at painting and was afraid to try. This made Michelangelo angry. He made up his mind he would show that he could do the work as well as any painter in the world.

First of all, he had to have a scaffolding built in the chapel. The scaffolding was a wooden framework with boards across the top near the ceiling so that Michelangelo could climb up on the boards and paint.

If you stop to think a moment, you will see how hard it must have been to paint pictures on a ceiling. The painter had to lie on his back on the scaffolding. He had to be so close to the ceiling that he could see only the part right above him, unless he climbed down the ladder and looked up. The ceiling of the Sistine Chapel is very large. The pictures on it had to be large so people could see them plainly from the floor down below. How would you like to draw the head of a man when you could not see where his feet were to be?

But once he had started, nothing could stop him. At first he had some other artists to help him, but he found the helpers couldn't do the work just as he wanted it, so he sent them away and kept on all by himself.

It took him four and a half years to finish the ceiling, and that was really a very short time when you think of the work that had to be done! The pope kept telling him to hurry and Michelangelo even moved his bed into the chapel so he would be able to spend more time painting.

The pope also kept telling him how the pictures should be done. Michelangelo didn't like this, because he felt he knew more about such things than the pope did. So one day when the pope was standing on the floor calling up advice to the painter, Michelangelo let a hammer drop from the scaffolding. He was careful to let it fall quite near the pope—near enough to scare him. After that the pope stayed out of the chapel while Michelangelo was painting!

Finally, the ceiling was almost finished. Michelangelo wanted to add some touches of gold paint, but the pope was so anxious to have the chapel opened that the artist had the scaffolding taken down before the gold was put on.

Then people came from all over Rome to see what the famous sculptor had done as a painter. What they saw was a painting of Bible pictures. Around the edges of the ceiling were huge figures of prophets who had foretold the coming of Christ. Down the middle of the ceiling were shown pictures of the Old Testament stories—The Six Days of Creation, Noah's Ark and the Flood, and others. The pictures were drawn so well that people were astonished.

The men and women painted on the ceiling look strong and solid. They look like statutes, which of course are the shape of real people all around, and not just flat pictures. So we call Michelangelo's paintings *sculpturesque* or like sculpture.

A small part of the ceiling shows the *Creation of Man*. Notice what great shoulders and muscles Adam has.

Almost thirty years after the ceiling was painted, Michelangelo was asked to paint a picture on the wall over the altar at one end of the Sistine Chapel. The wall was already covered with a painting by Perugino which had to be destroyed. Michelangelo's painting that took the place of Perugino's is called *The Last Judgment*. It is one of the most famous pictures ever painted, though it is not so great as the six ceiling pictures. It is crowded with the figures of men and women rising from the dead on judgment day.

Michelangelo painted very few other pictures. The only small finished painting that we are sure was done by him is a tondo, *The Holy Family*. It shows the Madonna on her knees, holding over her shoulder her little son so that Joseph can see him. The picture shows how this artist liked to paint people in strange positions.

Michelangelo lived to be a very old man. As he grew older he seemed to grow crosser and harder to get along with than ever. But though he was a cranky old fellow, everyone respected him and admired him as one of the greatest artists in the history of the world.

Leonardo da Vinci

Put this line in front of a mirror and then you can read it quite easily. ꙅƚᴎ⊥ ◁Ɐ⨱ᴚ ∩ⵒY ᴎɐɔ

That is what people found they had to do with notes written by a very great man named Leonardo da Vinci (Lay-o-nar'doe dah Vin'chee). But it is not because he wrote from right to left across the paper that we call him a very great man! It is because he knew how to do more things well than nearly anyone else in the whole world. Probably he wrote from right to left because he was left-handed.

Leonardo da Vinci lived in Italy during the Renaissance. He was born some years before the painter Raphael, and died a year before Raphael died. Painting was one of the many things Leonardo da Vinci did well.

One of Leonardo's paintings is in the Louvre, an art gallery in Paris. The picture is called *Mona Lisa* (Mo'nah Lee'sah). Some years ago this famous picture was stolen right from the wall of the Louvre and newspapers all over the world printed the story with headlines as big as if a great king had died or a big ship had been sunk at sea. Luckily, it was found and put back in the Louvre, though the thieves were never caught.

The *Mona Lisa* is a picture of an Italian woman. On her face is a faint smile. If the artist had changed the painting the least bit, there might have been no smile at all. It is a puzzling smile. Mona Lisa seems to be smiling at something that no one else knows anything about.

Leonardo da Vinci, **Self-Portrait,** red chalk, Imperial Library, Turin

There are other things to notice besides the smile. Notice how solid the woman seems—not flat, but as if she were a real person. Leonardo could make her look real because he understood how to use dark and light, how to make the bright part fade into the shadows. He was the first painter to understand how to do this.

Next notice the background, the part of the picture behind the woman. It is a landscape, with a stream and hills and mountains. When you look at a real landscape, you know you can't see things far away quite as clearly as things close to you. Leonardo da Vinci was a great enough painter to make the landscape look as if it really were far away. He was the first painter who understood how to do this, too.

Another painting by Leonardo is not in an art gallery, where it would be carefully taken care of, but is in a low, damp room in a monastery in Italy where it has been badly damaged by moisture. It is one of the world's greatest paintings, but it will never be put in an art gallery, because Leonardo painted it directly on the wall.

The picture is known as *The Last Supper*. It shows Christ and the twelve apostles seated at a long table. Leonardo chose to picture the moment when Christ has just said, "One of you will betray me!"

Can you not imagine how absolutely terrible to these apostles would be the thought of betraying their beloved master? Leonardo shows by their gestures, their hands, the expression of their faces, how each apostle feels when he hears these words.

To show what men in a painting *feel* is not easy. A painter cannot, of course, make the people in his pictures *speak* what they feel. If he wants to show their feelings, he must do it by showing how people look when they are thinking a certain thing. Leonardo visited deaf and dumb people, to learn how they showed their feelings when they were excited or happy or frightened or angry. This helped him make the people in his pictures show just the feelings he wanted them to—even if they could not speak.

Not many years after *The Last Supper* was painted, the paint began to come off the plaster of the wall. One reason for this was that Leonardo painted on the dry plaster. Michelangelo and other wall painters always had painted on the plaster when it was still fresh and damp. When they did this, the paint sank into the fresh plaster and *couldn't* peel off unless the plaster

Leonardo da Vinci, **Mona Lisa**, Louvre, Paris

66

Leonardo da Vinci, **The Last Supper,** Santa Maria delle Grazie, Milan

Leonardo da Vinci, **The Virgin of the Rocks,** Louvre, Paris

came off, too. You remember I told you this kind of painting is called fresco, which is the Italian word for fresh. Leonardo was interested in trying new ways of painting, and so, unfortunately, he didn't use the old-style fresco way for his *Last Supper*.

When the paint had flaked off in many places, other artists painted over the picture where they thought it needed touching up. After a time a great part of Leonardo's painting was covered by the much poorer painting of these much poorer painters. Worst of all, the monks decided to cut a door in the wall. The top of the doorway was made right in the middle of the lower part of the painting, and of course the hammering to make a hole through the stone wall jarred off more of the paint.

Later, Napoleon led his armies into Italy, and some of his soldiers used the room of *The Last Supper* as a stable for their horses! They even amused themselves by throwing their boots at the painting to see if they could hit Judas Iscariot, the apostle who betrayed Jesus.

So year by year this wonderful painting became more and more a ruin, until there was danger that it would be lost altogether. Finally, a wise Italian found a way of making what was left cling to the wall so it would not come off. Then he managed to take off all the paint put on by the other painters, so that now the picture is in better condition than it has been for hundreds of years.

We have only about three or four other paintings by the great Leonardo da Vinci. One that everyone likes is called *The Virgin of the Rocks*. It shows the baby Jesus and his mother seated on the ground with the little Saint John and an angel. They seem to be in a place of caves and dark rocks. Through openings in the rocks we can see the bright blue of a waterfall and the green of plants.

Leonardo knew more about plants and flowers than any one else of his time. One of the paintings of a follower of his named Luini (Loo-ee'nee) is named for a flower. It shows a young woman holding a columbine, so this painting is called *The Columbine*. Luini's women have the same kind of half-smile that Leonardo painted so well. Luini was a good painter, but not nearly so good as Leonardo da Vinci, the wonderful genius whom he imitated.

Leonardo da Vinci, **The Virgin and Child with St. John the Baptist and St. Anne,** study in charcoal and white, Royal Academy, London

Venice is a city where the streets are water and where you take a boat instead of an automobile to go from place to place. Today Venice belongs to Italy, but in the time of the Renaissance, though Venice was in Italy, it didn't belong to Italy. There wasn't any republic of Italy then, and Venice was an independent state, a republic that governed itself. Venice had its own army and navy, its own ruler called the doge, and its own way of doing things. It had its own great painters, too, during the Renaissance—painters still famous above all others for the wonderful colors they gave to their pictures.

In the early years of the Renaissance there was a painter of Venice named Bellini (Bel-leen'ee). He had two sons who also became painters. The sons were better painters than their father. One of the Bellini brothers taught painting to two young men who became better painters than any of the Bellinis. These two men were called Giorgione (Jor-jone'ay), which means Big George, and Titian (Tish'an), which just means Titian. Three Bellinis, Giorgione, and Titian—five men with only three names to remember.

I wish I had room to tell you more about the Bellinis. I think you would like their pictures of the doges, the rulers of Venice. But there isn't room in this chapter for all of them, so we'll begin with Giorgione.

Six Great Artists from Venice

Giorgione is called one of the greatest of painters. Like Leonardo da Vinci, he left very few pictures that we are sure he himself painted. A famous painting called *The Concert* is thought by most people to have been painted by Giorgione, but others think it was painted by Giorgione's friend Titian. *The Concert* shows the head and shoulders of three men. One of these men is seated at a clavichord. A clavichord is a musical instrument like a piano that was used before pianos were invented. The second man has a violin in his hand, and the third wears a big hat with feathers on it that makes him look like a woman.

Unfortunately Giorgione didn't live long enough to paint many pictures. A terrible disease called the plague spread through Venice. Giorgione caught the plague and died when he was only about thirty-two years old.

His friend Titian lived to be a very old man, and had time to paint many more pictures than Giorgione. Titian was especially good at painting portraits of the noblemen of his time. One of these portraits is called *The Man with the Glove.* No one knows who the man with the glove was, but almost everyone likes the picture.

Titian could paint other kinds of pictures besides portraits. He painted a picture for an altar in a church in Venice called *The Assumption,* which shows the Madonna entering heaven. The Venetians liked it tremendously. They especially liked its rich glowing color, for Venice itself was full of color, with its deep blue sea on every side and its marble palaces gleaming in the brilliant sunlight.

Venetians even liked pictures painted on the outside of their buildings, to add to the bright colors of the town. Both Giorgione and Titian made many paintings on the outside house walls, but all these have now been washed away by the weather.

At last, after a long life of painting, Titian died—some say from the same disease that had killed Giorgione, the plague.

There were still great artists left in Venice, however. One of these was called Tintoretto, which means Little Dyer, because his father was a dyer. Tintoretto was much younger than Titian. When he was still a boy he was sent to Titian's studio, or workshop, to learn painting. For some reason Titian let him stay at his studio for only ten days and after that Tintoretto had to teach himself to paint.

He too painted many pictures on the outside walls of buildings, but these have washed away like Giorgione's and Titian's. Titian had always been careful to make good bargains when he sold his paintings, but Tintoretto didn't seem to care for money. He was satisfied to take much less for his pictures than they were worth. Often he even gave them away.

One of Tintoretto's greatest undertakings was to paint pictures for the walls of a building called the Scuola di San Rocco in Venice. Michelangelo had made his wall paintings on wet plaster, Leonardo had made his on dry plaster, but Tintoretto made his on canvas. Then the canvas with the painting on it was fastened to the wall.

Tintoretto used to make little clay figures to use as models when he painted. He worked very quickly and was able to paint a great many pictures in his lifetime. Most of them are full of energy and action. Some of his figures seem to be rushing through the air. So much action and movement made his pictures very different from the quiet ones of early Italian painters. Tintoretto's were more like Michelangelo's energetic paintings. But Tintoretto also had the glowing colors of Titian.

Over his studio door he put these words: "The drawing of Michelangelo and the color of Titian." Sometimes he went beyond Titian, whose colors were golden browns and rich reds and greens. Tintoretto's later pictures contained soft shades of gray and had a silvery finish rather than a golden glow.

One of Tintoretto's famous paintings is called *The Miracle of Saint Mark*. The story goes that Saint Mark had a faithful servant who was sentenced to be tortured to death for being a Christian. Saint Mark was away when this happened. The servant was stretched on the ground in front of the judge's chair and the torture was about to begin. Suddenly the tools broke in the executioner's hands as Saint Mark appeared in the air above. He had come to save his servant.

Tintoretto's picture shows Saint Mark rushing through the air above the executioner, but nobody in the picture, except a little baby, has noticed him. All are looking at the broken tools of the executioner.

When Tintoretto was an old man he was given the order to paint a huge picture of paradise. The picture was to be large enough to cover a wall space thirty feet high and seventy-four feet long. Tintoretto set to work and finished the largest painting on canvas in the world. His *Paradise* shows Christ and the Madonna seated on clouds in heaven. Below them are crowds of saints and angels, over five hundred figures altogether. This painting was Tintoretto's last great work. He died soon after finishing it.

Some of Tintoretto's paintings were much better than others. The Venetians used to say he had three pencils, one of gold, one of silver, and one of iron. By this they meant that some of his pictures were wonderfully done, some were only fairly well done, and some were poorly done. Perhaps this is why people have had so many different opinions about Tintoretto.

Venice had great painters after Tintoretto. But certainly the Bellinis, Giorgione, Titian, and Tintoretto are enough great men to squeeze into one little chapter!

Titian, **The Man with the Glove,** Louvre, Paris

Art Reference Bureau

75

Tintoretto, **The Miracle of St. Mark,** Galleria Accademia, Venice

Titian, **Head of an Old Man**
Louvre, Paris

Titian, **Ranuccio Farnese**

Titian,
**Cardinal
Pietro
Bembo**

Andrea del Sarto, **Sacrifice of Abraham**

Andrea del Sarto, **Study for St. John**, British Museum, London

Del Sarto and Correggio

Andrea, whose father was a tailor, was a famous painter—one of the Renaissance painters of Florence. Italians, of course, didn't use English words for the painter's name. They called him Andrea del Sarto, which is the Italian way of saying Andrea of the Tailor.

When this son of the tailor grew up he married the widow of a hatter—a man who made hats. She was a beautiful woman but was always scolding and was very extravagant and selfish and spent Andrea's money as fast as he could make it.

Two of Andrea's paintings were sent to France and when the king of France saw them, he wanted the painter to come to France and paint for him. So to France Andrea went. The king was pleased with his work and paid him well, but soon Andrea got a letter from his wife telling him to come back to Italy. The king made him promise he would return to France very soon and gave him money to buy some pictures in Italy to bring back to France.

And now we see that Andrea's pictures were better than he was, for Andrea was what we call a "weak" man. When he got home to Italy, his wife made him build her a fine house. And when Andrea found his own money wasn't enough for the house he used the king's money! Of course, after such dishonesty, he was afraid ever to go to France again.

In Italy, Andrea painted several pictures in fresco on the walls of monasteries. You remember what fresco painting is. The artist painted on the plaster while it was still wet so the colors would soak into the wall. If a painter made a mistake in fresco painting, he couldn't rub it out, because the picture was part of the plaster. So most artists touched up their fresco paintings after the plaster was dry. Andrea, however, never did this. He could paint so well that he didn't have to correct mistakes after the picture was finished.

Andrea painted in oil as well as in fresco. You remember, don't you, that the early Renaissance painters used to mix their paints with egg or glue? Then someone discovered that it was better to mix paints with oil, and soon all the painters were using oil paints except for fresco. In the old egg or glue way of painting artists had to paint on a board covered with a kind of smooth plaster called *gesso* (jes'so). With oil paints they could paint their pictures on canvas or boards without using gesso.

Andrea's most famous oil painting is a Madonna. The baby Christ is in her arms, on one side stands Saint Francis, on the other Saint John, with two little angels between them. The picture has a peculiar name. It is called *The Madonna of the Harpies*. Do you know what harpies are? Harpies are make-believe animals—birds with women's heads. The Madonna in Andrea's picture is standing on a block or pedestal which is decorated with two little harpies. That's why we call it *The Madonna of the Harpies*.

The Madonna in this picture is supposed to look like Andrea's wife. He painted her likeness in almost all his pictures, but when poor Andrea finally caught the plague and became very ill, his selfish wife was so afraid of catching the disease herself that she left him alone and uncared for till he died.

Andrea del Sarto was named for his father's trade. Now we come to a painter who was named for his home town. You remember Perugino, who was named for the town where he lived? Well, not a great distance from Perugia is the town of Correggio (Co-red'jo) where there lived a painter known everywhere by the name of *his* town. We don't know much about Correggio's life, but we can admire his pictures. Like Andrea del Sarto, Correggio painted both in fresco and in oils. All his frescoes are in the city of Parma, in Italy, where he worked on the cathedral and the churches.

The cathedral in Parma has a round tower on top called a cupola and Correggio painted a picture for the inside of the cupola. The picture was circular so it would fit into the ceiling of the cupola. As it could be looked at only from the floor below, Correggio decided to make the angels and other figures in the picture look like real figures flying through the air and seen from underneath. If you should look straight up and see an angel flying above your head you would see the soles of the angel's feet nearer to you than his head.

To paint a figure seen from below was something that very few artists knew how to do. Correggio first had a sculptor make some models in clay so he would know how people would look in these strange positions. The way he painted them we call foreshortening.

Correggio did other foreshortened cupola pictures. People who saw them didn't quite know what to make of them. It was such a new way of painting that at first it wasn't liked very much. One man said such a painting looked like a hash of frogs. But the painter Titian came to Parma and when he saw Correggio's cupola picture in the cathedral he said, "Turn the cupola upside down and fill it with gold and even that will not be the picture's money worth."

Correggio's oil paintings are noted for their wonderful light and shade. He was what we call a master of light and shade. The people in his paintings are graceful, smiling, pretty, and happy looking. Almost everybody likes them. The main fault people find with them is that they do not seem to *mean* very much. Correggio was not a great thinker like Michelangelo and Leonardo da Vinci.

One of Correggio's paintings is called *Holy Night* or *The Adoration of the Child*. It shows the baby in his manger with his mother and the shepherds around him. A wonderful glow of light comes from the manger where the baby lies, and lights up the faces of those who worship him.

A strange story is told of Correggio's death, but whether it is true or not we do not know for sure. According to this story, Correggio was paid for one of his paintings all in bronze coins. You know that if you pay in pennies for something expensive, it takes lots of pennies. And this payment to Correggio took so many bronze coins that it made a very heavy load. Correggio started out to carry this load of coins home. It was a hot day and the heavy load made Correggio so hot and tired that he became ill, had to go to bed, and soon died. And that was the end of this master of light and shade. But his paintings have lived on after him to give pleasure to all who see them.

opposite left: Correggio, **The Virgin Adoring the Child**
Uffizi, Florence

———————————————————————

opposite right: Andrea del Sarto, **Madonna of the Harpies**
Uffizi, Florence

83

Flemish Art

———————

Do you know what a Fleming is? It isn't some strange animal you can see in the zoo. In fact, a Fleming isn't any stranger than you are, yourself, for a Fleming is a Flemish person—a person of Flanders. The strange thing about a Fleming is that he is also bound to be either a Frenchman or a Belgian or a Dutchman, as well as just a Fleming, for Flanders is now partly in France, partly in Belgium, and partly in Holland.

An interesting thing about the Flemings is that they had great artists who were painting at the same time as the early Renaissance artists in Italy. There were many more artists in Flanders at that time than there were in any other country except Italy. If you want to look up this country of Flanders on the map, look for Belgium. You will find it along the North Sea.

The first of the famous Flemish artists were two brothers named Van Eyck (Van Ike). Hubert was the older brother and Jan the younger. They worked in the city of Bruges, which is not a very important city now but then was one of the largest and richest cities in Europe. For a church in Ghent these two brothers painted a magnificent altarpiece. An altarpiece was not like an ordinary picture. An altarpiece had a central panel with wings or shutters on each side, like a threefold screen. These shutters could be closed like the shutters of a window, so the Van Eycks painted pictures on the back as well as on the front.

———————

Jan Van Eyck, **Jan Arnolfini and his Wife**
National Gallery, London

Hubert was the one who planned the paintings on this altarpiece, but before he had finished them all he died, and Jan completed the work. The altarpiece was so much admired that several cities wanted it for their museums. So it was taken apart and for a long time the central part was in one city and each of the shutters in another. After World War I the pieces were brought back to Ghent to make a complete altarpiece.

The altarpiece is almost all we have to show us how good an artist Hubert Van Eyck was, but Jan's paintings have been better preserved and there are several very famous ones in museums. Both the Van Eycks painted with oil, and they used oil so well to bring out the colors and to keep the paintings fresh-looking that the story soon grew up that they were the inventors of oil paintings. This isn't exactly true, but they did improve oil painting so much that we can call them the fathers of oil painting. From them the Italians learned to paint with oil.

The Van Eyck brothers were followed by other good painters in Flanders, but I'm going to have to skip them and tell you about the greatest Flemish artist, who lived two hundred years later than the Van Eycks. So that you'll know the time this was, I'll tell you that he lived from 1577 to 1640. His name was Peter Paul Rubens.

Peter Paul must have been a very bright boy, for he learned to speak Latin, French, Italian, Spanish, English, German, and Dutch! Do you know anybody who can speak seven languages?

As a young man Peter Paul worked for several years in Italy, for one of the dukes there. The duke liked his work so much that he would not give Rubens permission to leave. One day, however, Rubens had a message from Flanders telling him his mother was very ill. He started for home at once without waiting to get the duke's permission.

The rulers of Flanders were glad Rubens had come back and they not only gave him orders for pictures but made good use of him in other ways. He was entrusted with important missions to carry out in Spain, in France, and in England. Every place he went he won friends. The king of Spain made him a knight. The king of England made him a knight. Honors were heaped upon him. He continued to paint hundreds of pictures. In his house was a huge studio, where many young artists helped him as they learned from him. He liked to paint big pictures

Peter Paul Rubens,
Little Child Taking Its First Steps,
Louvre, Paris

Peter Paul Rubens, **The Artist's Sons,**
Leichtenstein Gallery, Vienna

best and the stairway of his studio was made very large so that his largest paintings could be taken from the studio after they were painted.

Rubens is noted for the rich, bright colors of his paintings. He could paint all kinds of pictures—portraits and landscapes, animals and battles, religious pictures and pictures of mythology and history. Some are so full of action they make you excited just to look at them. *The Lion Hunt* is one of the exciting ones. It shows men on horseback with spears, attacking lions, and the picture quickly shows you hunting lions is not a sport for weaklings. Rubens learned to draw lions by hiring a real live lion for a model.

Like most painters of his time, Rubens didn't mind painting people of the past in the same kind of clothes that people wore in his day in Flanders. No one then seemed to think it was peculiar to see a painting of an ancient Greek in the costume of the Flemings of the seventeenth century, but painters these days always try to have their figures wear clothes that would have been worn at the time the subjects were supposed to have lived.

---

opposite left: Peter Paul Rubens, **Self-Portrait,** drawing in red and black chalks, retouched with a pen by a later hand
Albertina, Vienna

---

opposite right: Sir Anthony Van Dyck, **Self-Portrait,** etching

Many people consider Rubens's masterpiece to be *The Descent from the Cross*. It shows Christ's followers removing his dead body from the cross on which he died.

A picture nearly everyone likes is the painting Rubens did of his two sons (page eighty-six). The older boy was eleven and the younger boy seven when Rubens painted their portraits. They look very lifelike, don't they? Indeed they look very much like boys of today except that their clothes are not the kind boys wear now even when they are dressed up to go to a party, or to have their pictures taken.

Rubens was not lazy. He worked hard and fast, but even then he had orders for more pictures than he could do. Sometimes he let his pupils paint parts of his pictures, to save time and also to give them practice. He was always ready to help

Sir Anthony Van Dyck, **Portrait of Charles I,** Louvre, Paris

91

other artists and sometimes bought their pictures only because they needed money. He even bought some of the paintings of a certain artist who had been very unfriendly to him, just because he felt sorry for him.

Rubens taught so many young men in his studio that some could hardly help becoming famous painters too. The best painter of all who studied under Rubens was Anthony Van Dyck (Van Dike). He went to England to live and painted there for the king, who knighted him for his work. Sir Anthony Van Dyck is most noted for his portraits of kings and noblemen and their families, but he also painted many religious pictures.

Sir Anthony Van Dyck became so famous at painting portraits of noblemen who almost all wore small pointed beards that even now we call a pointed beard a Van Dyck beard.

I wish I had room to tell you of other Flemish painters. With only this one chapter about them you may think Flemings are not so important in the story of painting as they really are. But I must tell you the last names of three Flemish painters who came between the time of the Van Eycks and of Rubens. They were a father and two sons and so all three have the same last name. The name is Brueghel (Brew'gal). I'm pretty sure you'll like their pictures. Look at them and see if you don't. The Brueghels' paintings are not at *all* like the Italian pictures.

above right: Pieter Brueghel the Elder, **Alchemist Laboratory,** engraving by J. Cock

below right: Pieter Brueghel the Elder, **Landscape with Country Dance,** detail, Uffizi, Florence

Two Dutch Artists

Next door to Flanders on the shore of the North Sea is the country called the Netherlands—the country of wooden shoes and windmills, of tulips and hyacinths, of the Zuider Zee, of canals and dikes.

The Dutch, like the Italians and the Flemish, had a Renaissance too. The Dutch Renaissance was later in coming than the Italian and the Flemish, but when it did come it produced some of the very best artists of the world.

The Dutch artists painted pictures that were different from those of the Italians and the Flemish. The Dutch religion had become a Protestant religion instead of Roman Catholic, and the Dutch did not believe in decorating their churches as much as the Catholics did. The Dutch artists, therefore, painted very

---

Rembrandt van Rijn, **Young Girl at an Open Half-Door**

few religious pictures, few Madonnas and holy families. Instead they painted portraits and landscapes and pictures of the everyday people and things they saw around them.

Their pictures differed in other ways too. In the older paintings of Italy and Flanders, for instance, most of the people in the pictures wore a natural expression on their faces. You can think of one of these artists saying to someone who was having his portrait painted, "Now just sit still and don't move, and I'll paint your portrait." But some of the Dutch artists had a different idea of portrait painting. A Dutchman named Frans Hals painted portraits of people who you know were not told to sit still and look natural. The expression on the faces of Frans Hals's portraits is what we call a fleeting expression. He caught a smile, or a grin, or a scowl—expressions that last only a second or two—and he made his pictures look as though in another second the expression would change.

Some pictures by Frans Hals were different in still another way. They showed the strokes of the paint brush not smoothed out, but left in the paint, as if the artist wanted you to see that he had painted the portrait quickly and caught the fleeting expression on the face with a few strokes of his brush. Not all his pictures are like this. Some are just as smoothly and carefully finished as can be. A portrait called *The Laughing Cavalier* is one of his most famous pictures. It shows the lace on the man's cuffs done very carefully—and lace is not an easy material to paint in a picture.

Another picture by Hals will show you the quick brush-stroke work that he could do so well. It is called *Malle Babbe* and shows a woman and her parrot. The parrot looks very much like an owl and the old woman isn't a bit pleasant looking. Sometimes the picture is called *The Witch of Haarlem*. Haarlem was the Dutch city where Hals lived.

Now, at the time Frans Hals lived and painted, the Netherlands had recently become a free and independent country. To make sure that they would be strong enough to keep this freedom from other countries the Dutch had bands of citizens who were trained to act as companies of soldiers in case of need. Gunpowder and guns were still so new that some of these companies still called themselves *archers* or crossbowmen. The officers of each company usually had their portraits painted all in one picture. Hals painted several group portraits of the archers and other companies. He is generally spoken of as the greatest of all Dutch portrait painters with the exception of Rembrandt.

This master, Rembrandt, did most of his work in the city of Amsterdam. He did not paint only portraits. He painted almost every kind of subject an artist could paint. Rembrandt created a light in his pictures that was unlike real daylight or lamplight but which makes his pictures marvels of brilliant light and deepest shadow. For years he worked hard, lived happily, and earned money and fame. But he spent so much money in collecting beautiful things he liked that he finally owed more than he could pay. His pictures became unpopular, too, and he found it hard to make money in his old age.

You wouldn't think, would you, that a picture that is now considered one of the great pictures of the world would be laughed at and disliked, and would make the painter unpopular when it was painted? But that is what happened when Rembrandt painted his *Night Watch. The Night Watch* was ordered by one of the companies of men who acted as guards for the city in time of danger. It was to hang in their club house and each member of the guard was to pay his share for having the picture painted.

Rembrandt wanted to show the stir and excitement as the guards marched out, and he painted the picture with the captain and his lieutenant in the front and the members of the guard hurrying out behind them with guns and spears. Children are there to watch the show, and even a dog appears in the picture. The light is very bright on some of the figures and the rest are in the darkness of night. The light is so different from ordinary light that some think the picture is a daytime scene and should not be called *The Night Watch*.

Now, when the members of the guard saw the picture, they did not like it.

"We paid to have our portraits painted," they said "and here the artist has stuck us in the background where it is so dark we can hardly even be recognized."

Other Dutchmen laughed at the picture. "We can't tell whether it represents night or day," they said. And from that time on Rembrandt sold fewer and fewer pictures.

Wouldn't you like me to show you a list starting with the very best artist in the whole world and then giving the second best and then the third, and so on down to the twentieth or fiftieth or hundredth best artist? Well, I'm not going to show you any such list, not because I don't want to, but because no one in the world can make such a list. If I did, it would be only my private opinion. It wouldn't be the best artist and the next best and so on, but the artist *I* think is best and the one *I* think is next best. And just because I think he's best doesn't mean he *is* best. No one artist is so much greater than all other artists that every one can say, "He is undoubtedly the best."

But if all the men who know most about such things made their own private lists of the best, I'm pretty sure all the lists would have Rembrandt somewhere near the top.

above right: Frans Hals, **Malle Babbe**

---

below right: Rembrandt van Rijn, **Portrait of the Artist**

Artists of the German Renaissance

"Don't forget to dot your *i*'s. Be sure to cross your *t*'s." Has your teacher ever said that to you? I always used to have a hard time remembering to dot all the *i*'s when I wrote compositions at school. But suppose I had gone to school in Germany. *There* the school children have to be careful about dotting *u*'s as well as *i*'s! For in Germany there are two kinds

above: Albrecht Dürer, **The Painter's Father,** National Gallery, London

below: Hans Holbein the Younger, **Edward VI as Prince of Wales**

opposite: Albrecht Dürer, **Adoration of the Magi,** Uffizi, Florence

PARVVLE PATRISSA, PATRIÆ VIRTVTIS ET HÆRES
ESTO, NIHIL MAIVS MAXIMVS ORBIS HABET.
GNATVM VIX POSSVNT COELVM ET NATVRA DEDISSE,
HVIVS QVEM PATRIS, VICTVS HONORET HONOS,
ÆQVATO TANTVM, TANTI TV FACTA PARENTIS,
VOTA HOMINVM, VIX QVO PROGREDIANTVR, HABENT
VINCITO, VICISTI. QVOT REGES PRISCVS ADORAT
ORBIS, NEC TE QVI VINCERE POSSIT, ERIT.

Ricard Morysini Car

of *u*—a plain *u* like ours, and a *u* with two dots on it like this, ü. A *u* with two dots is sounded something like our *u* in *pure*.

I wanted to tell you about the dotted *u* right at the beginning of this chapter because it appears in the name of the German artist Albrecht Dürer. His name, you notice, is not Durer but Dürer. He lived and painted at the same time as Titian, Tintoretto, Michelangelo, and Leonardo da Vinci. In fact, he knew some of the great Italian artists personally, for he took a trip to Venice and stayed there for some time. Germany was having a Renaissance as well as Italy and Flanders and later the Netherlands, and Albrecht Dürer was the great artist of the German Renaissance.

Dürer didn't paint much like the Italians. He painted many kinds of pictures, but his portraits are more famous than his other paintings. Besides paintings, Dürer made engravings. To make an engraving the artist cuts the lines of a picture in wood or copper. Then he puts ink in the lines and presses the wood or copper on a piece of paper. The picture that is printed this way is an engraving.

Dürer made many engravings. In fact, he is as well known for his engravings as for his paintings. Some of his engravings —the one called *Melancholy*, for instance—are as well known all over the world as his best paintings.

Dürer's woodcuts also are rightly famous. A woodcut is just the opposite from an engraving. The lines are drawn on the wood and then the wood is cut away from the lines, so that the lines are left raised. Then the raised lines are inked and pressed on the paper.

Hans Holbein the Younger, **Edward VI as a Child**

When Dürer made the trip to Venice that I mentioned, he was welcomed and honored by the Venetians as a famous man. The Venetian artist Bellini, who was then an old man, asked Dürer one day if he would give him one of the special brushes he used to paint the hair in his portraits. Dürer said, "Certainly," and gave Bellini the brush he was using.

"Why," said Bellini, "this is just an ordinary brush. Do you really paint those wonderful hairs with a brush like this?" Then Dürer took the brush and with it painted some hairs as only he could paint them.

Dürer admired the works of the Italian painters, but when he returned to Germany he continued to paint in his own way.

Albrecht Dürer painted several portraits of himself. He was able to do this, of course, by looking in a mirror and painting what he saw in the glass.

Dürer often put a great deal of detail into his pictures. He filled the paintings with all kinds of odds and ends, and every tiny button is painted as carefully as if it were as important as the person's face. Most of the German artists did this and in most of their pictures so much detail is a drawback. Your eye is drawn from the important things to the unimportant ones. But although Dürer often had just as much detail as other German painters, he was a great enough artist to keep the little things in the picture from becoming too important.

The second great Renaissance artist of Germany also was a portrait painter and a maker of woodcuts. His name was Hans Holbein (Hole'bine) and we have to speak of him as Hans Holbein the Younger because his father was also an artist named Hans Holbein.

The Holbeins moved to Switzerland, the country of the Alps, and Hans Holbein the Younger became the friend of a very famous man who lived there—Erasmus. Erasmus was a great thinker and writer. Holbein painted five portraits of Erasmus. One of them shows a side view of Erasmus—a profile. Erasmus sits writing at his desk. There do not seem to be very many details in this portrait, but in another famous portrait by Holbein, called *Portrait of Georg Gisze*, there are many things beside Georg Gisze himself. And yet, like Dürer, Holbein was able to keep them in their place so that after all Georg is the chief thing your eye looks at. Indeed, he left the unimportant details out of the faces of his portraits, putting in only the lines that would tell most.

Holbein found his business of painting was not doing so well in Switzerland, so he decided to take a bold step. He would go to England and see what work he could get there. He got a letter of introduction from Erasmus and went. The English liked his work and he painted portraits of most of the important Englishmen of the time including the king, Henry VIII.

Jan Vermeer, **The Lace Maker,** Louvre, Paris

Jan Vermeer of Delft

All any one knows about the life of one of the very great painters of the world can be written in a few sentences. Most great painters have had whole books written about their lives, but there isn't enough really known about the life of the Dutchman Jan Vermeer (Ver-mair') of Delft to make even a few pages. Here is almost all we know about him:

Jan Vermeer was born in Delft in 1632 and died there in 1675, leaving a widow and eight children. There it is in one

106

Jan Vermeer, **Lady Reading a Letter,** Galerie, Dresden

Jan Vermeer, **View of Delft,** Mauritshuis, The Hague

sentence—the life of Vermeer of Delft. Nobody even knows how many pictures there are that he painted, for some pictures we think he painted may have been painted by someone else.

But the pictures that we are sure were painted by him are considered very wonderful. Most of these are of indoor scenes. Only two, as far as we know, are outdoor scenes. Most of these paintings show a woman doing some very usual thing, like reading a letter or sewing or playing the clavichord or sometimes just looking out of the window. Perhaps his wife or one of his daughters posed for Vermeer's pictures. In some pictures there are two women and in a few there are men.

The wonderful way Vermeer could paint light coming into a room through a window is one of the first things people notice about these paintings. Next, one notices how well Vermeer could show what material a thing is made of—its texture. The lace cuff, the silk dress, the wooden chair, the silver pitcher, the ripe fruit, the shiny drinking glass, the pearl necklace, the blue china plate, are done so well that no one could doubt what each is made of. One could almost tell how each object feels to the touch. And over all streams the daylight from the window, binding the parts of the picture together. Some people say it is the finest daylight that any painter has ever put into an indoor scene.

One of Vermeer's pictures shows merely a woman reading a letter by a window, but it is painted so well that it has become famous.

Vermeer did not seem to have any imagination. He painted only what he saw. He never, for instance, made his women prettier than they really were. I don't believe he could have painted a dragon, or Saint George either, without looking at a real dragon (as if there were such a thing!) or at Saint George himself.

Why is so little known about so fine a painter? It seems mysterious, doesn't it? Vermeer's pictures were liked at the time they were painted, but then for some reason they were almost forgotten for about two hundred years. No one took the trouble to write down anything about the artist. Then his pictures were "discovered" again and became so valuable that it took a great deal of money to buy one. Most of Vermeer's paintings are now kept very carefully in museums.

This chapter is far too short for so important a painter. But there aren't any stories to tell about him unless I just make them up. Vermeer didn't use his imagination in painting his pictures, and I'm not going to use mine in telling you made-up stories. We'll just have to let Vermeer's pictures speak for him.

Spanish Artists

This chapter is about Spain. But I'm going to begin by telling you about Crete, which hasn't anything at all to do with Spain.

Crete is an island south of Greece. It belongs to Greece and the people of Crete speak the Greek language. Sometime about the middle of the fifteen hundreds (nobody knows just when) there was born in Crete a baby who was to become a celebrated painter. You probably have never heard his real name. I'll tell it to you, but don't try to remember it, for this painter is never spoken of except by his nickname. His real name is Domenico Theotocopuli.

He was a mysterious kind of man and no one knows very much about his life. He seems to have left Crete and gone to Venice to study art under the great Titian. The next we hear of him he has bobbed up in Spain and settled in the city of Toledo. In Spain he remained and in Spain he died in 1614, but he always thought of himself as a Greek rather than a Spaniard, and he signed his most important paintings in Greek letters. The Spaniards could hardly be expected to call him Domenico

Theotocopuli any more than you are expected to. They just called him "that Greek fellow" or "the Greek," which in Spanish is El Greco (El Gray'ko).

El Greco painted pictures that are so different from other artists' paintings that you may think they are not beautiful when you first see them. All his people are too long and thin to be like real people, and the colors are used differently from the colors in most paintings.

When you see a picture by El Greco you must remember that he is not trying to make you see a picture of things as they would look in a photograph. His paintings of men and scenes represent the spirit (or the idea), which is a different thing from what you would see with your eyes if you looked at real men and scenes. This is hard for many people to understand. They think a painting should always show you exactly what the real things look like. But a camera can do *that* just as well as an artist, and so many artists, like El Greco, sometimes paint not what they see but what they think will look best as a picture.

When El Greco died the man who was to become the greatest Spanish painter of all was still only a boy of fourteen. It seems strange to us that he is called by his mother's name instead of by his father's. It was just an old Spanish custom. I don't expect you to remember this painter's entire name, because it was Diego Rodriguez de Silva y Velasquez. What you have to remember is the Velasquez part, for that is what he was called. Velasquez (Vay-las'keth) was born in the city of Seville in 1599, the very same year that Van Dyck was born in Holland.

When Velasquez had grown up and had painted for some time he decided to go to the capital of Spain, Madrid. The king saw some of his work and liked it, and so the next year Velasquez was sent for and moved to Madrid for good. There he became the king's painter. We know very well what this king of Spain looked like, because Velasquez painted many pictures of him. That was one of the duties of the king's painter. The king was Philip IV. The first thing you notice about Philip is his very large mustaches which curl up to his eyes. They must have been a nuisance, those mustaches, for Philip had to put leather cases on them at night to keep them shaped right. I wonder what the king looked like when he got his fancy mustaches caught in the rain!

Velasquez,
Portrait of Philip IV
National Gallery, London

Velasquez, **Aesop**
Prado, Madrid

Velasquez, **Las Meninas (The Maids of Honor),** Prado, Madrid

113

Almost all the portraits of the king and his nobles show a wide stiff white collar that sticks out from around each man's neck. King Philip was very proud of this kind of collar, and for a very special reason—he invented it himself! He was so proud of his new invention that he had a great celebration after which there was a solemn procession or parade to church to thank God for such a blessing.

Velasquez was very different from El Greco in his painting. El Greco painted things as he wanted them to look, to give his idea of them. El Greco used his imagination instead of putting down on canvas just what he saw with his *eyes*. But Velasquez painted objects to look like the real objects. We call a painter who does this a realist, because he paints only what he really sees.

When Rubens came to Madrid, the king asked Velasquez to show him the art treasures of Spain. Rubens and Velasquez got along together very well. Rubens admired Velasquez's paintings and Velasquez admired the work of Rubens.

Velasquez wanted to see the famous paintings of the great Italian artists and so he got permission from the king to make trips to Italy, where he made copies of some of the paintings of Tintoretto, Michelangelo, and Titian.

And he painted a picture of Æsop, who wrote the fable of the Fox and the Grapes, the Dog in the Manger, and other famous fables.

Of course the picture is not of the real Æsop. Velasquez just painted the picture as he thought Æsop might have looked, for Æsop himself lived two thousand years before Velasquez.

Velasquez has been called the painters' painter, because so many painters have admired and praised his work. He was the greatest of the Spanish painters, greater than El Greco and greater than the next Spanish painter I'm going to tell you about, whose name was Murillo (Moo-reel'yo). Murillo, like Velasquez, was born in Seville. He went to Madrid, where

114

Velasquez encouraged him in his painting and got him permission to study the paintings in the king's picture gallery. After two years there, Murillo went back to live in Seville. He was still poor and unknown.

Now, about that time the Franciscan friars, or monks, in Seville were looking for an artist who would decorate one of their buildings with paintings. They wanted to get some famous artist, but they had too little money to pay a famous artist's prices. So they decided to let Murillo do the work. Murillo painted eleven pictures for the friars and every one liked them so much that he was asked to do more pictures than he could possibly paint.

Then Murillo painted eleven pictures for another building. These were even better than the first eleven, and made him famous.

Another picture that Murillo painted has a story told about it that shows how lifelike it is. The picture is of a priest with a spaniel at his feet, and the story is that when a live dog saw the painted spaniel he thought it was a real spaniel and growled at it. It reminds us of the story of the birds who pecked the grapes in Zeuxis's picture. I don't believe it can be a true story because a dog can't be fooled by a picture the way he can by a mirror.

Murillo was so successful at selling his pictures that he made a large fortune, but he was a very generous man and gave much money to the poor. He had once been poor himself, and he knew how much they needed help.

One day when he was old he was getting up on a scaffolding to paint the higher parts of a large picture, when he stumbled and fell. He was so badly hurt that he never got well and the picture was left unfinished.

The people of Seville never forgot their famous painter and even today in Seville they call any beautiful picture a "Murillo."

Murillo,
A Girl and her Duenna

Murillo,
The Young Beggar
Louvre, Paris

El Greco,
**Saint Martin
and
the Beggar**

Jean Antoine Watteau, **Italian Comedians**

Landscapes and Signboards

Fire escapes are part of the scenery in a city. Landscapes *are* the scenery in the country. Fire escapes have nothing to do with painting. Landscapes have a great deal to do with painting. But once upon a time landscapes had as little connection with painting as fire escapes have now.

It seems strange that from the time the cave men made their animal pictures thousands of years ago, all the way up to the middle of the seventeenth century, almost no one in Europe painted a real landscape. Italy had great painters during the Renaissance. Italy had beautiful landscapes. But strange to say the great painters never thought of painting the beautiful landscapes. If there was any country scenery at all in the Italian pictures, it was always as a mere background for the figures in the foreground.

The Van Eycks in Flanders had come near to real landscapes in their famous altarpiece. But the things happening in their picture were more important than the scenery.

Some landscapes had been painted in Germany about 1500, but they didn't attract much notice.

It seems strange that the first two painters of Italian landscapes were not Italians but Frenchmen. One was named Nicolas Poussin (Poo-sanh). He was interested in the stories of the ancient Greeks and in the old Roman ruins. His pictures usually have Greeks in the foreground, but the backgrounds are true landscapes. One picture shows the Greeks. It is called *Shepherds of Arcadia.*

Do you know where Arcadia is? Arcadia used to be a country of ancient Greece noted for its kind, happy, simple country people and shepherds. These shepherds that Poussin painted seem to be talking about a marble tomb in the picture. One is pointing to some words on the tomb. The words mean, "I too have been in Arcadia."

The other French artist who painted landscapes in Italy is known as Claude Lorrain. His real name was Claude something else, but as he came from Lorraine, in France, he is always called Claude Lorrain. The story goes that he was once a pastry cook and later the servant of a painter in Italy. One of his duties was to clean the paint brushes of his master. This interested him in painting. His master gave him some lessons and soon Claude Lorrain was a painter himself.

Claude Lorrain painted people in his pictures, but usually they were small and unimportant. The landscape was the important thing—even more important than it had been with Poussin. So Claude Lorrain is sometimes called the father of landscape painting. He liked to paint pictures of the sea even more than landscapes, so we might call him a seascape painter too.

The next important French painter lived about a hundred years later than Poussin and Claude Lorrain. His name was Watteau (Wah-toe). One of his paintings was on wood and was painted as a signboard for a hat shop. Poor Watteau led a miserable life. In the beginning he was very poor. When he came to Paris to paint he worked hard, but he was paid so little he almost starved. At last, when he had become well known as a painter and was making enough money to live comfortably, he was always so ill that he could not enjoy himself much, and finally he died of the disease that had made him ill.

The pictures Watteau painted are just the opposite from sad. The people in them are just the opposite of the kind of person Watteau was.

Instead of painting poor people, he painted young men and women clothed in silks and satins.

Instead of painting hard-working people like himself, he painted only people having a good time.

Instead of painting ugly, crude people like himself, he painted people who are almost too graceful and pretty and polite.

Chardin (Shar-danh) was another French painter who was born only a little later than Watteau. He too painted a signboard. Perhaps he got the idea from Watteau, but Chardin's sign was for a surgeon's office instead of for a hat shop. It showed a crowd of people in a street looking on while a surgeon binds up the wound of a man hurt in a sword fight.

Chardin liked to paint still life. Still life means a picture of anything without life such as fruits, dead fish, basins, cut flowers, dead rabbits or pheasants and other game, pots, pans, and so on. He was also a portrait painter. But the third kind of painting that Chardin liked to do is the kind he is best known for—scenes of people inside their houses, doing the everyday things that people do. Usually there are children in these pictures. One painting shows a mother teaching her little girls to say grace before meals, another shows a little boy spinning a top on a table, another shows a mother telling her son to be careful of his new hat when he goes out.

Though the people in Chardin's time dressed differently from us, we can say when we see his paintings. "Those look like real everyday people." We feel he didn't try to show us something astonishing or exciting, but just ordinary scenes in ordinary French families.

Jean Baptiste Siméon Chardin, **Blowing Bubbles**

INDEX: *Young People's Story of Fine Art, 15,000 B.C.-1800 A.D.*

———————

Type   *Century Expanded*
Typesetter   *American Typesetting Corporation*
Printer   *The Regensteiner Corporation*